THE HALLOWEEN RETROSPECT
VOLUME THREE

EDITED FOR THR ARCHIVE LIBRARY
BY ROBERT AARON WILEY

Copyright © 2024
First Printing, June 2024, 100 copies.

∞

Insert A: Poster - Haunted House Timeline: Hallmark 1950-1980
Insert B: Puzzle Bulletin, Frolic I - Crossword: Afterworld Lodger

∞

Cover: Gibson pop-up c. 1968 c/o THR. Photograph by Robert Aaron Wiley.

ISBN: 978-0-9836300-4-3

THE HALLOWEEN RETROSPECT
PO Box 963
Placitas, NM 87043

https://halloweenretrospect.com

THR does not employ AI-generative technology. Content herein is created by human biological entities to ensure the results engage accurate research with mindful artistry.

Hallmark centerpiece envelopes (left to right, top to bottom) **1:** *175HCP2-5E Witch and Haunted House Centerpiece* **2:** *150HHD2-4 Pre-Assembled Home Decoration "Haunted House"* **3:** *150HCP10-9 Plans-a-Party "Pop-Up" Decoration "Graveyard"* **4:** *100HCP1-2 Plans-a-Party Halloween Decoration* **5:** *100H103 The Hallmark Haunted House* **6:** *125HCP8-9 Plans-a-Party Pop-Up Decoration "Haunted House"* **7:** *150HCP7-2 "Pop-Up" Decoration "Witch"* **8:** *125HCP3e Ambassador "Haunted House" Pop-Up Decoration* **9:** *125HCP1-3 Plans-a-Party Centerpiece "Haunted House".* ∞

CONTENTS

Letterbox / Introduction   4

Halloween Haunts - Part 1   8
the witch's cottage and spook house additions

Halloween Haunts - Part 2   15
engineered mansions and hallmark innovations

Haunted House Timeline   25
hallmark haunted houses 1950-1980: poster & key

Haunted Vinyl   27
sound effects recordings from the 60's & 70's

The Catalog Audience   29
the context of readership to define content

Index   31
the halloween retrospect, vol. 1 - vol. 3

LETTERBOX

LETTERS

The Halloween Retrospect welcomes comments and questions but please note that such a print forum will follow traditional requirements for rationale and references, while slight editorial adjustments may be requested to fit the format.

Please send your correspondence (including name, hometown, and state) via letter carrier to *The Halloween Retrospect*, ATTN: Letterbox, PO Box 963, Placitas, New Mexico 87043. Email may be sent to letterbox@halloweenretrospect.com.

If you find your letter turning into a submission, then by all means read further...

SUBMISSIONS

While this publication inevitably begins as an isolated operation, it is with great awareness that numerous open minds, and open sources continually advance our knowledge with illuminating clues about the vintage world. Therefore, following are guidelines for submitting expertise as an article:

- **Content**: Vintage Halloween circa 1900-1979 is favored but there is consideration for submissions (of collectibles, holidays, etc.), with crossover interest.
- **Citation**: Verifiable primary sources are necessary to provide less speculative content, and see **Introduction**: **Regarding**: **Sources** to learn more about these requirements. There is no minimum.
- **Credit**: As with citation, please provide credit where due to identify owner and/or source for quotations or examples (images, etc.).
- **Length**: No limit is set (yet) but this small (novelty style) publication benefits from brevity, so 500+/- wordcount is adequate particularly when images are included.
- **Biography**. Please include an additional short paragraph or two about yourself. This does not count against any word limits.

See above for the applicable address to send both letters and submissions.

Introduction

STATEMENT OF INTENT

The Halloween Retrospect approaches vintage Halloween collectibles through the perspective of vintage market material to create citable data analysis. (For more on the history of THR and other author projects, please see ***THR, V1***: Introduction).

As before, guidelines for research articles are:

- **Question everything, and play devil's advocate.** Vintage collecting finds all of us, expert or not, discovering clues from the past. The policy of this publication will be to examine sources and question assumptive second-hand information.

- **Observations over expectation, and acceptance of the challenges.** Building on the previous point, the content cannot flinch from idiosyncratic facts or the surprising anomaly, even should this astonish the author and disrupt the field of collectibles.

- **Disagreement encouraged, but provide sources!** Again, content and analysis are based on tangibles. Disagreement is welcome, but arguments (perhaps as a letter or submission) should be supported with primary, not secondary, sources.

As well, the publication will attempt to follow certain inclusion/exclusion rules:

- **No reference as to identify a specific item for sale.** All too often a remark (even an aside) becomes part of the sales environment, skewing a +/- market. Commentary will avoid this, and future trade will be a separate pursuit rather than promotional.

- **No reference as to identify specific buyers or sellers.** When social privilege is metered for value (in either direction) rather than the collectible as an independent object, this too skews a +/- market and clouds deeper understanding.

- **No top ten playlists nor holy relics.** Every collector has a bias based on personal experience of a circumstantial market. Content here will attempt to find a broader picture rather than a single voice expressing the hype of sudden novelty.

Also, the following are important disclaimers:

- **THR does not employ AI-generative technology.** All content is created by human biological entities to ensure results engage accurate research with mindful artistry.

- **Outdated and insular concepts and beliefs expressed by vintage materials** do not reflect author, contributors, publisher, nor anyone involved in the final product.

REGARDING SOURCE

Source is a topic *The Halloween Retrospect* continues to contemplate across its duration per content that references an at-hand archive library of vintage publications. Therefore, it is meaningful to examine source - differentiated in research terms as primary or secondary. Whereas a primary source offers data in its initial form, a secondary source is removed from that original data by offering derivative/interpretive content. While it might be argued THR volumes are also secondary, they distinguish themselves by using primary sources constantly and conspicuously for the reader.

To date, most books of Halloween collectibles are surveys (and secondary as defined). Therefore, outcomes are similar with each displaying a range of content helpful for product identification. One can scour such books for visual and tactile information, and enjoy (when that author is affable and forthright) the sharing of experiences. However, readers may forget that unless cited (which is rare to none) that certain content is filtered by degrees of bias. For example, can one guide be truly omniscient when a person has two dozen items unseen by another? Perhaps then, one should instead consider greater perspective on rarity or on valuation (price and/or artistic merit).

For vintage Halloween collectors, secondary sources include the following:

‣**Pamela E. Apkarian-Russell "Collectible Halloween with Values"** (1997) and **"More Halloween Collectibles: Anthropomorphic Vegetables and Fruits..."** (1998)

‣**Dan Campanelli "Halloween Collectibles: A Price Guide"** (1995)

‣**Mark B. Ledenbach "Vintage Halloween Collectibles: 3rd Edition"** (2014)

‣**Charlene Pinkerton "Halloween Favorites in Plastic"** (1998)

‣**Stuart Schneider "Halloween in America: A Collector's Guide with Prices"** (1995)

While the above books are recommended for the reference shelf, diligent collectors can find more transparent publications of historically-sourced information. From the modern era, two books are most useful to *The Halloween Retrospect*.

‣**Claire M. Lavin "Timeless Halloween Collectibles: 1920-1949"** (2005) is distinct by way of content obtained through in-person visits to a single archive, The Beistle Company. The scope results in a focused survey of classic designs with behind-the-scenes data such as, for example, a product's release year. That said, collectors with broader tastes must bolster this source by other means.

Note: Lavin followed with **"Time for Halloween Decorations"** (2007), and for more on Beistle see Jeannette Lasansky **"Collecting Guide: Holiday Paper Honeycomb: Cards, Garlands, Centerpieces, and other Tissue-Paper Fantasies of the 20th Century"** (1993).

‣**Ben Truwe "The Halloween Catalog Collection: 55 Catalogs from the Golden Age of Halloween"** (2003) is distinct from other survey books as a compilation of vintage catalog publications (1919-1971) both vendor and consumer. This provides a direct view of the past market. That said, this inspiring anthology is more powerful to readers who take initiative to connect threads across pages and beyond.

THR's ARCHIVE LIBARY

Following the examples of Lavin and Truwe, *The Halloween Retrospect* leans toward the minority end of the reference shelf. Foregoing the showcase appeal of rarity, price, merit, etc., these volumes will instead lean toward meticulous analysis on featured subjects. Therefore, the research will originate by way of trade-specific publications (for manufacturer, distributor, and consumer) of traditional formats, books to pamphlets, from 1900 to 1979 (depending on the conversation).

THR library sources, as of this volume's release, include the following information objects that directly portray Halloween consumer goods of the vintage market:

‣ **540** publications consisting of 249 hardcopies and 291 digital surrogates

‣ **456** publications with definitive dates, with 73 crude and 11 a bit obscure

‣ **100** professional entities from the U.S. with 6 from other countries

‣ —? (uncounted) incidentals: books, magazines, advertisements, etc.

These numbers evolve as does the library, and every accession reaches for a goal of precision. Exact dates, for example, control an item's value as an authoritative primary source. While many publications are marked with a noticeable copyright, others require scrutiny. One means of verification examines a catalog's place within the company's print history. Timelines for catalogs may surprise us, for example, when edition/volume numbers are inconsistent. Further, date authentications do not rely solely on reverse logic, that is, dating a source by contents; this misplaces both the collectible and the container (i.e. catalog) to fit a pre-imagined interpretation both static and stubborn.

So, what does such stringency achieve? For an example of authoritative primary sources pursuing an item's written record, rather than second-hand information, please read further. Articles here are sure to illuminate as well as stoke further inquiry. And now, on to the shelves...

Halloween Haunts - Part 1
The Witch's Cottage and Spook House Additions

INTRODUCTION

Cottages that skulk in the rustling weeds of neglected lots... mansions that brood among the shadows of contorted forests... these are but a sample of cursed architecture described in countless stories: around a glowing campfire... against the static of olde time radio... within the cold glitches of digital streams. The haunted house is requisite habitat for Halloween's phantasmagoria quietly awaiting, oh foolish mortals, for us to enter if we dare! Yet, in what era do these ramshackle frames with grimacing physiognomy gain significant visibility among other seasonal collectibles? Imagine a time before card companies circa 1950's (as Hallmark) realize the haunted house can go from support role to headliner. Part 1 (of this two-part article) is an abbreviated look at the beginnings of an early-20th-century to mid-century transformation for the haunted house as an expression of Halloween.

THE WITCH'S COTTAGE

Based on THR's library of field guides that survey the early years of Halloween products, there are a few examples of the haunted house as diecut, candy container, or lantern. Compare this to a saturation of jack o'lanterns, black cats, witches and more. It seems instead, along with corn fields and cemeteries, that these eerie abodes are relegated to background (often as warmly-lit cottages) residing in postcard ephemera or book and magazine illustrations. However, since many of the on-hand book surveys are non-cited, there is a question of incidental bias. Perhaps a perceived infrequency may

Witch cottages frequent Halloween ephemera in the twenties. A fortune (p. 8) of a set by Whitney c. 1926 is available a number of years through various school suppliers. Dennison (p. 9) offers the H567 Night Scene place card (1928-1930) and their 1924 Bogie Book illustration is given a new version on the cover of a 1930's price list (p. 9). All items THR.

be cross-examined through a single company's output - and Dennison makes a great choice as both idea-maker and product creator with abundant output particularly during an apparent publication peak (***THR, V2***) 1912-1935.

First, in Dennison articles, it is evident ghostly locales are essential, yet text and imagery are targeted on party devices and tableaus of home, school, church, dancehall. Thus, while mantel, window, and performance stage are steeped in seasonal trappings, the haunted house by name is rather slow to coalesce. Browsing titles as early as 1912, it is possible "The Halloween Party in Your Home" (*Bogie Book,* 1923) hints at a conceptual shift as guests are led by "sheeted figures [with] radium stickers above each eye and on their finger tips" through dark trials to the main concern: the party. The next year's 1924 autumn annual contains a creepy illustration (on its Contents page) of a witch-hosted cottage, and in 1926 the series depicts a street-facing makeover to the home's front porch. Finally, Dennison in 1928 names the place in question with pamphlet "Investigating the Haunted House" while *Party Magazine: Vol. 1, No. 3* describes recognizable concepts to modern readers one-hundred years later with "A Spectral Spree" where The Haunted Corridor (see p. 10) is full of multiple scenes titled The Devil's Kitchen, The Chamber of Phantom Horrors, The Gray Mystic's Cave, and The Human Bone Heap.

Next up, review Dennison product lines in brochures, catalogs, and price lists. One will see examples of haunted houses present on seals, diecuts, and crepe..., but not of great number compared to the cast of more animated entities. And here once again it is the archetypal witch's cottage (that exemplifies the haunted house) on ephemera such as placecards (p. 9). None too different are Whitney (p. 8) and Beistle (p. 13) with neither veering far from fairytale expressions. It seems for Dennison, like others of the era, that a cottage is the predominant motif. However, this rather humble icon changes over the late twenties into the thirties. Halloween's haunted house is about to respond to certain cultural

9

*"**The Haunted Corridor**, [...] can be built along any route [...]. Stairways, either up or down, make ideal approaches. Rooms or closets that occupy strategic positions along the way can be used to tremendous advantage for Special Sights, [...], The Devil's Kitchen, The Chamber of Phantom Horrors, The Gray Mystic's Cave, The Human Bone Heap, [...]. The haunted corridor is merely a high, narrow aisle made chiefly of cornstalks and gaunt, bare branches, the latter hung with a gruesome sort of Southern moss which is really fringed gray crepe paper, with murkier shadows here and there fashioned of fringed black crepe paper, cut in ragged straggles. Peeping out along both sides of the aisle are assorted horrors, such as white skeleton heads, horrible dead hands and amputated long, thin, white legs. The hands are white kid gloves stuffed with sand, and the legs are nothing more deadly than a pair of sister's old white silk stockings filled with sawdust."* (Dennison, 1928)

demands, and as with "A Spectral Spree" there are certain stand-out occurrences of transformational haunts...

1) "The Haunted House Halloween Party" Entertainment Bulletin (by ELAINE promoted in a 1931 column of *Good Housekeeping*) offers a remarkably edgy depiction. Here, "the hostess will have great fun getting her haunted house ready for the visiting spooks," and in The Ghost Walk (section) portrays the now-familiar "long narrow hall [...] banked on each side with cornstalks and shrubbery behind which is concealed assistants who sigh, groan, shriek eerily and occasionally reach out a stark white gloved hand" in a scene completed with mechanical vermin and rubber bats. These suggestions are paired with an appropriately horrible illustration (p. 11) by Mabel Betsy Hill. The artist's visual is rendered as a chaos of black cats, jack o'lanterns, invasive skeletons, and a peek-a-boo ghost. And while broken shutters and a tattered fence are definitely not *good housekeeping*, the doorstep tombstone is particularly grim!

2) Despite apparent sparsity of portable haunted houses in earlier holiday markets, there are non-seasonal examples including "Caught in a Haunted House" by Toddy Inc. (p. 12). Absent from survey books of Halloween collectibles, it is not specific to the holiday, and yet like Cornish Litany imagery (not shown) anticipates a new demand

that Halloween haunts run amok with shadowing things from bats to witches.

Even with such examples of increased size, ghostly infestation, and frequency as a party theme manifestation, it appears that Halloween's haunted house is stubborn to change from party scene to party favor among the realm of marketable goods. Perhaps early-20th-century customers or companies simply prefer the cottage, but this author has not currently sought enough sources for an in-depth explanation. For the time being, this article recognizes companies of the era seem to create in mind of longevity such as Beistle (p. 13), and for more on shelf-life (including a remarkable item with a near 30-year run) read "Timeline for Witches" from **THR, V2**.

HOME IS WHERE THE HAUNT IS

Researchers (outside of this article's concern for ephemera) point to the 1930's as the era which likely produces our modern expectation of Halloween's haunted house. In *Trick or Treat: A History of Halloween*, Morton points to "rough beginnings in the 1930's, when parents, anxious to divert the attention of pranking boys, created events like 'trails of terror,'" and refers (p. 101) to *Hallowe'en Fun Book* of 1937 that describes "different parts of [a] maze [of] different themes: 'Ghoul's Gaol', 'Mad House', 'Tunnel of Terrors', and 'Dead Man's Gulch'." Readers here will recall "A Spectral Spree" yet that is now amplified with "a chair wired to deliver a mild electric shock, the rental of a creepy abandoned house [...], and 'Autopsy', [for a scene of] fake surgery."

Advice found in *Recreation, Vol. 32, No. 7* (National Recreation Association, 1938) backs Morton's assessment. "If it must be an indoor party, be sure to call it something attractive enough to lure the boys who want a good scare. Make it a 'Haunted House

> *Ideas for "A Spectral Spree" appear in Dennison 1928 (p. 10) and repeat in Plumb's own book "Here's for a Good Time" (T.S. Denison & Co., 1928). The book includes bits like "Halloween Horrors Party" and "A Halloween Hunting Party" (ending badly for a witch). The ideas are not unlike ELAINE's "The Haunted House Halloween Party" of Good Housekeeping, Vol. XCIII, No. 4, with art by Mabel Betsy Hill, 1931 (p. 11). These predict a more chaotic haunt like "Caught in a Haunted House" by Clay Weaver for Toddy, Inc. 1932 (p. 12), yet cottages for some persist for multiple seasons as with Beistle circa 1930's-1970's (p. 13). All THR.*

Cottages and shacks (above) persist with Beistle. The initial version of the witch's cottage (left) releases 1941 (Lavin, 2005) pitched as "new and swanky" in catalogs '48, '50, '54, '57-58, '58-59, and on? The 3-D cottage (right) releases in 1955 (Lavin, 2007) and monster shack (middle) in 1966 (Lavin, 2005). All items THR.

Party' - every community has a haunted house around some place - or a 'Spook Party,' or a 'Graveyard Party,' or a 'Witch Party,' (with Walt Disney realism if necessary, though not for small children), or a 'G-Men Party.' No party is spooky enough for 'Hallowe'en age' boys unless it has a Chamber of Horrors or a Trail of Terror." With how-to's for creating these scenes, the piece concludes, "a full evening of specially planned *gorified* entertainment such as this, it is doubtful that many of the group will go *hoodluming* about after the party is over. They have had enough thrills for one night!"

As trends reach mid-century, could these various ideas inspire manufacturers to reach beyond shanties and instead explore multi-room products engaging inventive material, scale, and interactivity? A sample of Halloween-specific items could include: (A) point-of-sale packages that wrap candies in haunted house facades with tinted cellophane-windows, as with Brach's Tricks or Treat Haunted House (circa 1954-1958 per ad sampling), as well as (B) the 1960's explosion of sound effects on vinyl records (p. 27) including, to name a few, *Spook Stuff for Hallowe'en* (MP-TV Services, Inc., 1960), *Sounds to Make You Shiver* (Soma, 1961), and *Chilling, Thrilling Sounds of the Haunted House* (Disneyland, 1964), or also (C) a growing use of mansion-type imagery in decor such as diecuts or with blow-molds such as Empire Plastics 1969.

From the examples directly above, Halloween's haunted house is becoming a hand-held item of great diversity, and in paper too. Compare them to earlier items as well as those arriving later - as paper travels well beyond flat surfaces and illustrated boxes. While some companies like Beistle (p. 13) continue older traditions, the consumer is about to experience a market of intricate holiday offerings with haunts ready to be spotlit in "Halloween Haunts - Part 2: Engineered Mansions and Hallmark Innovations."

HALLOWEEN HAUNTS - PART 1

SOURCES

Beistle Company, The. (1948). *Bee-Line Catalog*. [Including '50, '54, '57-58, '58-59]. Shippensburg, PA.

ELAINE. (1931). The Art and Etiquette of Entertaining, The Haunted House Halloween Party. For Bulletin Service of *Good Housekeeping XCIII*(4), p 11.

The Halloween Party in Your Home. (1923). In *Bogie Book* (pp. 2–3). Dennison MFG Company.

Lavin, C.M. (2005). *Timeless Halloween Collectibles 1920-1949, a Halloween Reference Book from the Beistle Company Archive with Price Guide*. Schiffer Publishing, LTD.

Lavin, C.M. (2007). *Time for Halloween Decorations*. Schiffer Publishing, LTD.

Morton, L. (2022). Trick or Treat in the New World, Halloween Haunts. In *Trick or Treat: A History of Halloween* (pp. 100–110). Reaktion Books, LTD.

Plumb, B. (1928). A Spectral Spree. In W. A. Norwood (Ed.), *Party Magazine: October-November* (II, Vol. 5, pp. 2–4). Dennison MFG Company.

Plumb, B. (1929). October. In *Here's for a Good Time: A Collection for Parties for Holidays and All Kinds of Miscellaneous Social Occasions* (pp. 186–213). T. S. Denison & Company.

Prescriptions for Hallowe'en Hoodlums. (1938). In *Recreation: October, 32*(7), pp. 385–387, 422-423. https://www.google.com/books/edition/Recreation/Xr0vAAAAYAAJ.

ILLUSTRATIONS

Beistle Company, The. (c. 1941-1968). *Embossed Halloween Plaque, Halloween Favor-ette and 3-D Fantasy*. [Decorations]. The Halloween Retrospect, NM.

Dennison Manufacturing Company. (1930) *Dennison's Price List Hallowe'en and Thanksgiving Decorations*. [Brochure Cover]. The Halloween Retrospect, NM.

Dennison Manufacturing Company. (1928-1930). Night Scene H567. [Placecard]. The Halloween Retrospect, NM.

Dennison Manufacturing Company. (1928). A Spectral Spree. [Illustration]. In *Party Magazine, Oct-Nov: II*(5), p. 2-4. The Halloween Retrospect, NM.

Hill, Mabel Betsy. (1931). The Witch of the Glen Gives a Party. [Illustration]. In *Good Housekeeping XCIII*(4), p. 11. The Halloween Retrospect, NM.

Weaver, Clay. (1932). Caught in a Haunted House. [Puzzle]. For Toddy, Inc. The Halloween Retrospect, NM.

Whitney. (c. 1926). The House of Fate [Mechanical Fortune]. The Halloween Retrospect, NM.

HALLOWEEN HAUNTS - PART 2
ENGINEERED MANSIONS AND HALLMARK INNOVATIONS

INTRODUCTION

Whether found in astonishing fiction or curious news clippings, the haunted house is non-exclusive to season or century. Thus, with or without October festivities, the place in question (see "Halloween Haunts - Part 1") enjoys broad appeal as from mid-century onward it transforms into a tangible collectible. Such non-seasonal merchandise from the period includes (as dated from advertisements) the Haunted House vertical-field electronic game in plastic (c. 1962-1966 by Ideal), and Hootin' Hollow Haunted House battery-powered push-button toy in metal (c. 1963-1967 by Marx). Also, it is worth noting The Haunted Mansion (Disneyland 1969 and Walt Disney World 1971) opens as next-level dark-ride entertainment offering year-round immersion. Yet, circling back to an emphasis on holidays, how fares the season-specific haunted house, particularly in traditional materials? What follows is a return to an earlier focus on paper in the hands of some very inventive card companies.

Above: front face (left) and pop-up detail (right) of greeting "Watch Out! It's Hallowe'en" 15H47 Norcross mechanical greeting card 4⅜" w x 5⅜" h closed, marked as gifted on October 31, 1952. The Halloween Retrospect archive collection.

15

Above: front (left) and pop-up detail (right) of greeting "HI! Happy Halloween!" 100H501 Gibson mechanical, litho in Japan, 7⅜" w x 9½" h closed, marked as gifted in 1968. The Halloween Retrospect archive collection.

NORCROSS & GIBSON

Reviewing THR's collection, the selections of at-hand items appear to characterize a mid-century revival of paper creativity that echoes the larger market's exploration of material, scale, and interactivity. Much ephemera of the period reflects a renewed interest in mechanics such as slot-and-tab assembly or pop-ups. As creators begin to experiment with three-dimensional architecture, objects begin to emerge beyond the static backgrounds that typify earlier works, and Halloween's haunted house begins to acquire a deservedly greater presence in items such as cards and centerpieces.

Examine the Norcross card (p. 15). While a shack is nostalgic, the building is integral to the inhabitant's forward action. It is great fun and the company will continue such exploration - including at least one haunted house assembly card (no date, not shown). However, Gibson of the 1960's goes further with a hectic residence expanding from the card's interior (p. 16 and cover). As well, their top-hinged slot-and-tab tent card (p. 17) offers a less-complex but similar effect. Each card tempts viewers into exploring various dimensions from surface to cut-aways, with surprising details awaiting inside and out. And yet another company goes further, for which the remaining article focuses.

HALLMARK CARDS, INC.

Hallmark (established c. 1910 and to date the largest U.S. card company in operation) at one time is yet another mid-century contemporary exploring ideas in paper goods (and business structure). Recalling this era, Hallmark stresses the company's know-

> *Above: front (left) with back detail (right) of greeting "Lots of love, Son. Boo to You!" 25H7160 3, Gibson dimensional slot-and-tab easel, 4¼" w x 6⅝" h closed. No marks. The Halloween Retrospect archive collection.*

how with dimensional products since the forties (Hallmark Cards, Inc., 1968). Yet, their article indicates another important factor which is Hallmark's support then for teams of *mad scientists* harnessing a synergism of art and engineering. The company allows these associates to pursue unlimited imagination, particularly by example (p. 18) with Howard Lohnes, Mechanical Designer. The results are past products that are today's collectibles, and THR will survey some rather revolutionary paper haunts 1950-1980. Readers are urged to explore images (here and on the blog) to fully grasp the extent of artistic ingenuity the company realized with their multi-faceted paper constructions.

RESOURCE NOTES

Regarding first a matter of sources, this author is thrilled to report that, unlike the fate of too many histories lost or buried, Hallmark maintains an intellectual fortune in its own private archive began in the fifties. Therefore, select data is available for which this author is grateful, as well as amazed that any amount is accessible given so narrow an inquiry compared to an immense product history! Yet as readers might guess, a bit of empathy is also requested given natural challenges that here include: 1) few company catalogs prior to the early seventies, 2) production/sale notation absent for certain items, 3) store records require non-corporate discovery, and 4) this author is simply too late to interview the creative minds from the era in question. Therefore, with apologies for any ambiguities, the analysis herein builds upon information by way of additional: 1) footwork outside of a single archive, with 2) questions to independent individuals, and 3) resourcing of external news and advertisements.

Howard Lohnes with Hallmark Cards, Inc. during the years 1946-1986 is shown, here in 1968 as lead of Mechanical Design, then 20 years with paper mechanics for the company. He states: "Some dimensional products require as many as seven specialists in different fields from chemistry (for glues, inks) to trigonometry (for curved folds)." And the article highlights a core group of twenty-five (up from two) including Mechanical Designers Bruce Baker, Marsha Bookwalter, John Garrison, Michi Kanelo ~ Design Stylist Dick Dudley ~ Design Specialist Jim Krekovich ~ Creative Design artist/designer Gayle Bergman ~ among others. That team's wealth of creative ideas such as "Halloween ghosts that pop up and say BOO!" are tempered by Lohnes explaining, "A new design may offer the most advanced mechanics and the latest high-fashion colors, but if it doesn't 'come alive' in the customers' hands when it unfolds we won't publish it." This is complicated by some designs too advanced for market, and yet the Hallmark line at one time could include over 300 mechanicals. (Hallmark Cards, Inc., 1968)

PRODUCT DATA & IDENTIFICATION

The Hallmark Archives (2023) indicate that products generally hit the past market one to a few years dependent on demand, including additional shelf-life possible through Ambassador (a 1959 debut for mass channel retail stores - grocery, drug, and women's department stores). However, apparent data cannot (as yet) offer official release dates nor inform us on strict moratoriums. To assist this situation, The Halloween Retrospect constructs a three-part blog series (see **Additional Reading**) which codifies external market evidence such as Hallmark's packaging evolution. Envelope designs together with advertisements make much discoverable, but lean toward Hallmark per their available newspaper campaigns compared to brands such as Ambassador.

For general package identification (1950-1980) one should expect: 1) a Hallmark/Ambassador logo, 2) item title and/or event/holiday, 3) item depiction as illustration/photograph, and 4) SKU. Other attributes may include: 1) copyright for Hallmark or for other intellectual licensing, 2) marketing campaigns like Hallmark Plans-a-Party or Ambassador Styles-a-Party, or 3) additional traits of text and layout, and for more on these, again readers should consult THR's blog for **Additional Reading**.

SKU = PRICE | TYPE | SERIAL

Hallmark archival staff (2023) interpret SKU (see back of envelopes pp. 22-23) as **sale price | event/product type | product/inventory number**, and note numerical skips or repeats will frustrate any obvious sequencing. In future perhaps author (or another) will create a spreadsheet for clues (as previously performed with serial numbers on Dennison publications in *THR, V2*) but until then, certain generalizations follow.

> **RETAIL PRICE:** While it is tempting to assign dates based on price, THR has no internal knowledge defining a standard system of cost, markup, etc., that encapsulates such amazing product variety. This means prices may rise or drop out of sequence, but one need not explain that prices increase over the decades.

The Hallmark Haunted House is early in product evolution of cards to card holders to table centerpieces, and appears in ad clippings circa 1954-1959. This non-assembled item is held at THR with a sales unit box marked **HU 103**. *THR archive collection.*

*Plans-a-Party is a Hallmark marketing campaign of coordinated party goods as with the set including **Halloween Decoration 100HCP1-2** (left) at THR. Multiples appear with store owner R. J. Dellenbeck (1961) in a photo care of Hallmark Archives.*

▸**PRODUCT TYPE:** Basically, this is an abbreviation with examples (below) that one might encounter for Halloween. Note that other events/holidays replace H, as in E for Easter, X for Christmas, or simply CP for a non-seasonal centerpiece.

H	Halloween
HCP	Halloween Centerpiece
HH / HHD	Halloween Home / Halloween Home Decoration
HHM	Halloween Home Mechanical (Decoration)
HYP	Halloween Youth Party / Partyware

▸**PRODUCT NUMBER:** Spaced or dashed, this requires further study. Hallmark archival staff (2023) ponder if a SKU such as **150HCP1-7** "indicates that six other designs proceeded" but notes it does not explain **Tom Cat Centerpiece 175HCP1-1** and **Scarecrow Centerpiece 175HCP1-1** both of 1972. Until more data, THR points to an important aspect of matching sets. **Haunted House 100H103** pairs to nut cup **HN103**, and tally **H 103T**, while Plans-a-Party owl centerpiece **100HHD2-5** pairs to nut cup **100HNC2-5**, etc. What more might we discover in future?

ENVELOPE DESIGNS

1950-1959: EXPANDING SEASON

Hallmark's work with paper products in the 1950's evolves beyond the company's dimensional work of 1940's greetings cards (pp. 17-18) toward a market introduction of card holders (as Christmas trains and sleighs). If one equates the scale of marketing for such designs with successful sales, Hallmark seems inspired to explore new creations of larger-scale paper throughout the event calendar. Circa 1954 they unveil **The Hallmark Haunted House** (p. 19), a spook-filled slot-and-tab centerpiece for Halloween parties. This is also notable in that the **HU 103** store unit (in the THR archive) is labeled to contain coordinated invitations, place cards, tallies, and nut cups.

1950's PACKAGES (p. 19) have the following qualities:
- White envelopes shift horizontal (p. 19) to vertical (p. 20) near end of decade.
- Early packages (p. 19) are optional mailers printed with postal data front or back.
- Product images change from illustrations (p. 19) to studio photography (p. 20).
- A white header-bar (p. 20) develops as primary location for logo, title, price, etc.
- Most products of this time are several pieces packaged for assembly by customer.

1960-1969: EXPANDING MOTIF

Hallmark's products during the 1960's literally unfold with vibrant imagery and multitudinous designs. Including such niche ideas as a dinosaur birthday theme with **Prehistoric Party 150CP163-2** (not shown), the result is too many Halloween products spanning the decade to fit this book. Thus, confining focus to haunted houses, one finds a Plans-a-Party **Halloween Decoration 100HCP1-2** (p. 20) arriving circa 1961 (and with Ambassador later) as a pop-up with minor assembly. Two years later, 1963's

Pop-ups by Hallmark **"Haunted House" 125HCP8-9** *(left) & Ambassador* **"Haunted House" 125HCP3e** *(right) from THR archive collection. Note that other ogle-inducing pop-ups (see poster) include* **"Witch" 150HCP7-2** *circa 1965-1969, and* **"Graveyard" 150HCP10-9** *circa 1967-1971. Howard Lohnes (p. 18) states in conversation with Montanaro (1993) that around thirty such pop-ups exist for various events.*

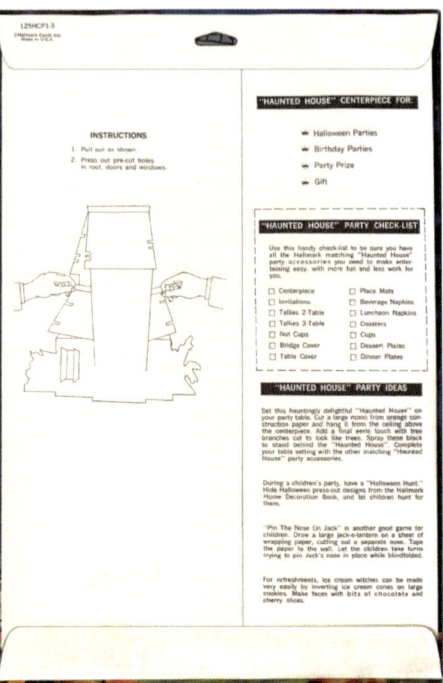

Above: Hallmark **"Haunted House"** *125HCP1-3 envelope (front/back) follows a basic sixties layout, and see THR's website blog for more details. THR archive.*

Haunted House 125HCP8-9 (p. 21) is offered, while a similarly styled but marvelously bonkers **Haunted House 125HCP3e** from Ambassador arrives somewhere around that time (based on the envelope). The decade also offers another Plans-a-Party piece circa 1966-1967 **Haunted House 125HCP1-3** (p. 22) as well as **Haunted House 150HHD2-4** (see poster) with the latter also of an uncertain date yet in line with envelope trends.

1960's PACKAGES (pp. 20-22) have the following qualities:
- White header (p. 20) vanishes early, replaced with full-bleed photography (p. 21).
- Logo, name/type, price, appear at top, at times with a list of corresponding items.
- Placed under Hallmark's logo, Plans-a-Party marketing (pp. 20-22) later dissipates.
- Back envelope (p. 22) is text-on-white assembly with party sets or suggestions.

1970-1979: EXPANDING FORMAT

During the 1970's, Hallmark's spirit for the haunted house, or perhaps its scarier aspects, appears to wander. The company continues Halloween pieces like **Witch and Haunted House Centerpiece 175HCP2-5E** (p. 23) and circa 1977 **Haunted House 250HCP29-2** (see poster) yet, as with **Happy Hauntings 250HHD801-3** (see poster) moods are whimsical. Also, the latter though labeled HHD is less seasonally specific given the absenteeism of jack o'lanterns. The same shift in mood and season is true with pop-up book *A Visit to the Haunted House* (1972) as well as puzzle **The House on Haunted Hill** (1973) via Hallmark's acquisition of Springbok. With Halloween no

22

longer required for these products, the company seems to discover (as in non-Halloween items p. 15) that haunted houses can be an all-year seller.

1970's PACKAGES (p. 23) have the following qualities:
- Logo, name/type, price, etc., move to top right of envelope's full-bleed front.
- Back envelopes highlight instructions on color upon the white background.
- Back envelopes shift to generalized copy less specific to matching sets.
- Later packages hint at 1980's graphic choices such as linear highlights (see blog).

WHAT NEXT?

From humble fairytale cottages in the scenery of small handheld ephemera (as by Dennison in "Halloween Haunts - Part 1") to the engineered castles that demand scrutiny in party centerpieces (as by Hallmark in "Halloween Haunts - Part 2") there is still much remaining for a full survey of Halloween's haunted house across ephemera. Until future volumes allow for further exploration expanding the focus of this two-part article, readers can enjoy more haunted houses in the next section "Haunted House Timeline" (p. 25 and an 11"x17" fold-out poster) that highlights Halloween paper goods from Hallmark 1950-1980. Travel the path, stamp your tickets at the doors, and send a dispatch or two about your discoveries for inclusion in a future volume.

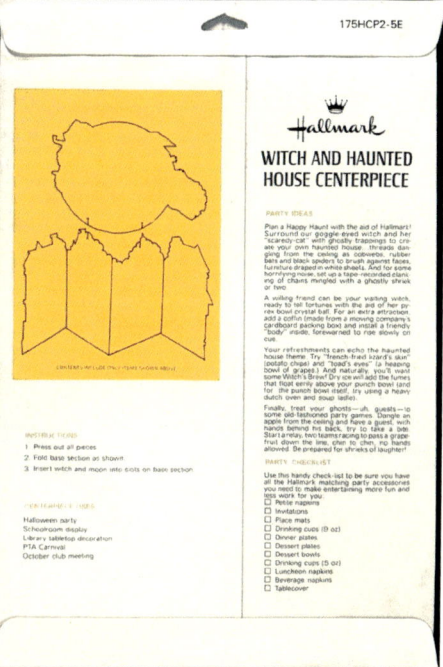

*Above: Hallmark **Witch and Haunted House 175HCP2-5E** envelope (front/back) follows a basic seventies layout, and see THR's website for more details. THR blog.*

HALLOWEEN HAUNTS - PART 2

SOURCES

Hallmark Cards, Inc. (1961). Flying High, Down South. *Cards Magazine, Autumn.* Kansas City, MO.

Hallmark Cards, Inc. (1968). And They Wiggle, Giggle, Wink, and Blink. *Cards Magazine, Spring,* 22–27. Kansas City, MO.

Hallmark Cards, Inc. (2024). Correspondence re: *Halloween Centerpieces and Table Decorations.* [List and Data]. Hallmark Archives. Kansas City, MO.

Montanaro Staples, A. (2006). Hallmark Pop-up Decorations. *Moveable Stationery, 14*(2), 6–8. https://ia804501.us.archive.org/21/items/movablestation1422006mova/movablestation1422006mova.pdf

ILLUSTRATIONS

Ambassador Cards, Inc. (c. 1960's). Pop-Up Decoration "Haunted House" 125HCP3e. [Envelope]. THR, NM.

Gibson. (c. 1968). HI! Happy Halloween! 100H501. [Greeting Card]. USA. THR, NM.

Gibson. (c. 1960's). Lots of love, Son. Boo to You. 25H7160-3. [Greeting Card]. USA. THR, NM.

Hallmark Cards, Inc. (c. 1954). The Hallmark Haunted House 100H103. [Envelope]. THR, NM.

Hallmark Cards, Inc. (c. 1961). Halloween Decoration 100HCP1-2. [Envelope]. THR, NM.

Hallmark Cards, Inc. (c. 1963). "Pop-Up" Decoration "Haunted House" 125HCP8-9. [Envelope]. THR, NM.

Hallmark Cards, Inc. (c. 1966). Centerpiece Haunted House 125HCP1-3. [Envelope]. THR, NM.

Hallmark Cards, Inc. (c. 1970's). Witch and Haunted House Centerpiece 175HCP2-5E. [Envelope]. In *Hallmark Halloween: 1970's.* The Halloween Retrospect. https://halloweenretrospect.com/hallmark-vintage-halloween-collectibles-part-three/

Dellenbeck, R.J. (1961) Flying High, Down South. [Photo: Hallmark store owner]. In *Cards Magazine, Autumn.* Hallmark Cards, Inc.

Lohnes, Howard. (1968). And They Wiggle, Giggle, Wink, and Blink. [Photo: Head of Mechanical Design]. In *Cards Magazine, Spring.* pp. 22-27. Hallmark Cards, Inc.

Norcross. (c. 1952). Watch Out! It's Hallowe'en 15H47. [Greeting Card]. New York. THR, NM.

ADDITIONAL READING

Hallmark Halloween: 1950's, Hallmark Halloween: 1960's, Hallmark Halloween: 1970's. The Halloween Retrospect [Blog entries]. 2024. https://halloweenretrospect.com/

Haunted House Timeline: Hallmark 1950-1980. The Halloween Retrospect [Poster Insert]. 2024.

Haunted House Timeline
HALLMARK HAUNTED HOUSES 1950-1980: POSTER & KEY

POSTER KEY

As an extension to "Halloween Haunts - Part 2" the following poster insert and key offers additional haunted house information for Hallmark's vintage decor pieces. See that article in *THR, V3* (pp. 15-24) for more on how such data is sourced.

- **A : 100H103 The Hallmark Haunted House**
  Circa 1954-1959
  Assembly: Height 10¼"
- **B : 100HC 11-1 Party Decoration for Halloween.** (Eerie Witch in 3-Dimension)
  Circa 1956-1958
  Assembly: Height 15"
- **C : 100HCP1-2 Plans-a-Party Halloween Decoration** (also Ambassador SKU?)
  Circa 1960-1961
  Pop-up w/some assembly: Height 11½"

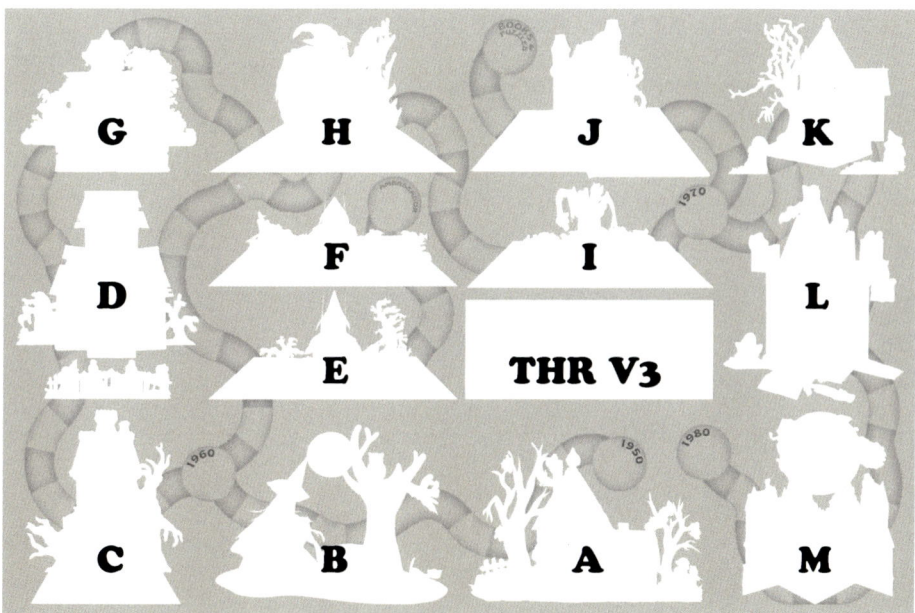

*Poster key for **Haunted House Timeline: Hallmark 1950-1980**. Items A to F and H from THR archive. Items G and I to M, faithful renditions pieced from digital data.*

25

➤ **D : 125HCP1-3 Plans-a-Party Centerpiece "Haunted House"**
  Circa 1966-1967
  Expandable w/some assembly: Height 12"

➤ **E : 125HCP8-9 Plans-a-Party Pop-Up Decoration "Haunted House"**
  Circa 1963-1967
  Pop-up: Height 11"

➤ **F : 125HCP3e Ambassador "Haunted House" Pop-Up Decoration**
  Circa 1960's
  Pop-up: Height 9½"

➤ **G : 150HHD2-4 Pre-assembled Home Decoration "Haunted House"**
  Circa 1960's
  Expandable: Height 11¾"

➤ **H : 150HCP7-2 "Pop-Up" Decoration "Witch"**
  Circa 1965-1971
  Pop-up: Height 10"

➤ **I : 150HCP10-9 Plans-a-Party "Pop-Up" Decoration "Graveyard"**
  Circa 1967-1971
  Pop-up: Height 8½"

➤ **J : A Visit to a Haunted House**
  ©1972 (with various editions into the 1980's)
  Pop-up Book

➤ **K : 250HCP29-2 "Haunted House" Centerpiece** (also Ambassador 259HCP6H)
  Circa 1977
  Assembly: Height 12⅝"

➤ **L : 250HHD801-3 "Happy Hauntings" Centerpiece**
  Circa 1970's
  Assembly: Height 14½"

➤ **M : 175HCP2-5E Witch and Haunted House Centerpiece**
  Circa 1970's
  Assembly: Height 16½"

Once again, for more about the data, read *THR, V3:* "Halloween Haunts - Part 2" (pp. 15-24) together with blog entries "Hallmark Halloween" (1950's, 1960's, 1970's).

SOURCES

Wiley, R.A. (2024). Halloween Haunts - Part 2: Engineered Mansions and Hallmark Innovations. In *The Halloween Retrospect, Volume 3*. Placitas, NM.

ILLUSTRATION

Wiley, R.A. (2024). Poster key for Haunted House Timeline: Hallmark 1950-1980 [Graphic]. The Halloween Retrospect. NM.

ADDITIONAL READING

Hallmark Halloween: 1950's, Hallmark Halloween: 1960's, Hallmark Halloween: 1970's.
The Halloween Retrospect [Blog]. 2024.
https://halloweenretrospect.com/vintage-halloween-collectibles-blog/

HAUNTED VINYL
SOUND EFFECTS RECORDINGS FROM THE 60'S & 70'S

Like games referred to in "Halloween Haunts - Part 2" (*THR, V3*), vinyl recordings epitomize late-20th-century exploration of material, scale, and interactivity. And those with sound effects, in particular, offer new ways to bring ghost-infested haunts *home for the holidays*. Readers will also notice that cover art parallels trends discussed in the aforesaid article; for example, compare the character count in the lingering solitude of Disney 1964 to 1977 (p. 27) to the crowded chaos of Pickwick 1974 (p. 28).

QUICK LIST

While numerous online audiophiles have given this topic ample sonic exposure, what follows is a starter-list (with release dates) of Halloween sound effects recordings prior to 1980. Creating this list (*using discogs.com*) it is worth noting that prior to the 1950's there are nearly zero examples of the genre whereas 1960 sets the model for years afterward. As well, a list reveals surprises. This author learns that a childhood 70's standard *Sounds to Make You Shiver* (p. 28) is originally released a decade earlier!

Though pulled from "Halloween Haunts" these covers are examples of Halloween's changing haunt imagery. Disney releases two (non-related) albums in 1964 (left, THR) and 1979 (right, discogs.com). Compare these to Pickwick's chaotic 1974 re-release (p. 28, THR) that in 1961 was a photo of skeletons in the home (?) at the piano, etc.

1960: *Howlin Hallowe'en: The Sounds of Spook Stuff* (MP-TV Services, Inc.)

1960: *Spook Stuff for Hallowe'en* (MP-TV Services, Inc.) - *same tracks as above*

1961: *Sounds to Make You Shiver* (Soma) - *see 1974*

1962: *Hallowe'en Spooky Sounds* (Sounds Records)

1964: *Chilling, Thrilling Sounds of the Haunted House* (Disneyland)- <u>not</u> *the '79 version*

1969: *The Story & Song from the Haunted Mansion* (Disneyland)

1971: *The Haunting* (Gayle House)

1973: *Ghostly Sounds* (Peter Pan Records) - *not related to the following*

1974: *Ghostly Sounds* (Power Records) - *not related to the previous*

1974: *Sounds of Terror* (Pickwick)

1974: *Sounds to Make You Shiver* (Pickwick) - *see 1961*

1977: *Halloween Horrors: Sounds of Halloween (& Other Useful Effects)* (A&M)

1977: *Sound Effects Vol. 13 (Death & Horror)* (BBC Records & Tapes)

1979: *Chilling, Thrilling Sounds of the Haunted House* (Disneyland) - <u>not</u> *the '64 version*

Since THR samples this list for a study of imagery rather than audio, it is likely not an exhaustive selection, and countless more recordings arrive after 1980. As well, the list neither pursues musical genres nor other oddities one might use to sonically accompany the holiday, but it is still a good place to start with most, if not all, found online. That said, for an authentic experience bring home some vintage vinyl for those warm analog pops as you imagine yourself lost in the details of the haunted house cover art. ෴

SOURCES

Discogs. (n.d.). Discogs: Music Database and Marketplace. https://www.discogs.com/.

ILLUSTRATION

Disneyland. (1964). *Chilling, Thrilling Sounds of the Haunted House.* [Cover Art]. THR, NM.

Disneyland. (1979). *Chilling, Thrilling Sounds of the Haunted House.* [Cover Art]. www.discogs.com/release/6662439-No-Artist-Walt-Disney-Studios-Chilling-Thrilling-Sounds-Of-The-Haunted-House

Pickwick. (1974). *Sounds to Make You Shiver.* [Cover Art]. The Halloween Retrospect. NM.

The Catalog Audience
THE CONTEXT OF READERSHIP TO DEFINE CONTENT

TERMS DEFINED

Acquiring vintage, one should note that original source materials (such as catalogs) are some distance removed from their previous owners who in turn are but one segment of that era's marketplace. This is important. For example, readers of *THR, V2*: "Skittle or Decor" witness the obscuring of title data as imports move from vendor to consumer. So, if today's collectors name an object based on vendor, does that reflect the reality of purchaser? Therefore, while absent at time of THR's previous volumes, it is worth catching-up on terms (dry good, general merchandise, jobber) in relation to audience (consumer, vendor, or other). Here is a useful list to consider:

- **Distributor**: This intermediate moves product from Manufacturer to Wholesaler or Retailer, thus a so-defined company catalog is likely aimed at other vendors.
- **Dry Good(s)**: Literally a non-liquid item, and in retail, a product neither hardware nor grocery. The term is less favored as offerings expand beyond such distinctions.
- **Favors**: Common to consumer or vendor, these are products often as gifts for use at parties. Note: Shackman suggests credit for term's popularity in an early catalog.
- **General Merchandise**: This like Dry Good(s) includes consumer good categories except hardware, grocery, or second-hand. It is common in retail and wholesale.
- **Gross**: Unit of measurement for 12 dozen (or 144 pieces) not often available to the average consumer, and likely indicates catalog's audience as market intermediates.
- **Importer**: Company providing foreign products to the catalog's market audience, that on its own does not define the catalog as aimed at consumer or other vendor.
- **Jobber**: A synonym for wholesaler (see below) often found on earlier catalogs.
- **Manufacturer**: The company which produced the product, and when viewing their material one must ask if the content is aimed at the consumer or an intermediate.
- **Novelty**: Common term on consumer or vendor catalogs, it denotes the decorative, humorous, transitory nature of an item not necessarily required in day-to-day life.
- **Premiums**: Items such as prizes (at carnivals, contests, etc.) which may be used as an inducement to gain further participation, particularly for additional spending.
- **Retailer**: Store or otherwise that directly sells products to the consumer market.
- **Wholesaler**: An intermediate participant that buys items (particularly in quantity) from Distributors, Manufacturers, etc., often as products then sold to retailers.

TERMS & RESEARCH

When approaching vintage publications, data collection would serve future research by recording terms (p. 29) perhaps apparent on: cover graphics, order sheets, business descriptions, or internal listings. As well, additional phrases not listed here may support a definition of source, for example, while consumers also want *great buys on sale*, words like *profits* or *money makers* are aimed at intermediates. Therefore, recording terms is helpful (again referencing the "Skittle or Decor" controversy) to researchers who may wonder about fickle product data as items move, for example, from intermediate suppliers (stocking with Gellman) to consumers (shopping at Shackman).

To close, there is certainly much more that is worth study on the subject of collectibles in relation to supply chains. And whenever such points seem important in future, THR will attempt to bring this data forward. In the meantime, hopefully closer examination of terms on sources may help with our modern interpretations.

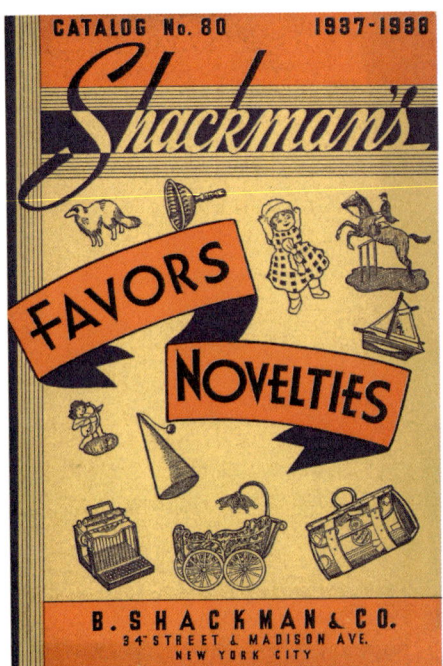 

B. Shackman & Co., No. 80, 1937-1938 (left) of numerous decades with a New York storefront offers favors with many imports to consumers. Gellman Brothers, No. 68, 1953-54 (right) represents a warehouse Importer and Jobber offering novelties (some in gross) to retailers. All items THR.

ILLUSTRATIONS

B. Shackman and Co. (1937-1938). *Shackman's Favors, Novelties. No. 80.* [Cover]. THR N M.

Gellman Brothers (1953-54). *Our Annual Buyers' Guide. No.68.* [Cover]. THR NM.

INDEX

THE HALLOWEEN RETROSPECT, VOL. 1 - VOL. 3

ARCHIVE

Framingham History Center	V2
Hallmark Archives	V3
History Colorado: Research Center	V1

ARTISTS / CREATORS

Hill, Mabel Betsy	V3
Lohnes, Howard (and Associates)	V3
Weaver, Clay	V3

AUTHORS / EDITORS

ELAINE	V3
Lavin, Claire M.	V1 - V3
Morton, Lisa	V3
Plumb, Beatrice	V3
Truwe, Ben	V1 / V2

COMPANY, Manufacturer

Beistle Co., The	V1 / V3
Brach's	V3
Dennison MFG Co.	V1 - V3
Disney	V3
Gibson Greetings, Inc.	V3
Hallmark Cards, Inc. (Ambassador)	V3
Ideal	V3
Marx	V3
Norcross Greeting Card Co.	V3
Pickwick	V3
Rosen (Rosbro)	V2
Toddy, Inc	V3
Whitney	V1 / V3

COMPANY, Retail

Einzinger & Co.	V1
Sears	V2
Shackman & Co., B.	V2 / V3

COMPANY, Trade / Wholesale

Gellman Brothers	V3
March Brothers Publishing Co.	V1
Paine Publishing Co.	V1
Western Novelty Co., Denver	V1

CODES & MARKS

Dennison, Publications	V2
Hallmark Cards, Inc.	V3
Imports, German	V1
Shackman & Co., B.	V2

ICONS & ENTITIES

Black Cat	V1 / V2
Ghosts	V3
Haunted House	V3
Jack O'Lantern (Pumpkin)	V1 - V3
Owl	V2 / V3
Skeleton	V1 - V3
Witch	V1 - V3

31

INSERTS (THR)

Post Cards	V2
Posters	V1 - V3
Puzzles	V3
Tally Cards	V1

NOVELTIES

Candy, Desserts	
Cake Embellishment	V2
Sucker Holders	V2
Treat Containers	V1 - V3
Costumes	V1
Decor, General	
Centerpieces	V3
Tableware	V2 - V3
Wall Plaques	V1 / V3
Diecuts (Flat, Embossed)	
American	V1 / V3
Beistle Co., The	V1 / V3
German	V1
Fortunes	V1 / V3

Games & Toys	
Metal	V3
Plastic	V3
Skittles	V2
Greeting Cards, *et. al.*	
Assembly	V3
Mechanical (Pop-Up, etc.)	V3
Lanterns	V1
Noisemakers	V1
Sound Recordings	V3

PUBLICATIONS

Bogie Book, *et. al.*	V2 / V3
Good Housekeeping (Bulletin Service)	V3
Narrenfibel (Karneval)	V1
Normal Instructor & Primary Plans	V1
Recreation (Nat. Rec. Assoc.)	V3
Shackman's Favors	V1 - V3
Teachers Catalog	V1
Teachers Year Book, The	V1
Western Novelty Co., Denver	V1

Made in the USA
Middletown, DE
04 July 2024